Also by Robert Milton

TIPS -- The Imaginative Parent Succeeds

Hole in the Soul (novel)

The unspoken (novel)

The True Believers (non-fiction)

*The Reach (*novel)

Flexxible Brain (non-fiction)

Woman Aware (non-fiction)

Numinous Mirrors (poetry)

NUMINOUS MIRRORS II

SCIENCE--THE POETRY OF NATURE

ROBERT MILTON PH.D.

authorHOUSE®

AuthorHouse™
1663 Liberty Drive
Bloomington, IN 47403
www.authorhouse.com
Phone: 1 (800) 839-8640

Published by AuthorHouse 03/20/2015

ISBN: 978-1-4969-7362-7 (sc)
ISBN: 978-1-4969-7365-8 (e)

Dedication

As often as one feels grateful to those who have 'labored', helped and facilitated in a book's publication, -- I could create an unending list here! -- In this case, I would like to dedicate these poems to the ever-growing cadre of 'awakening' adults who have discarded the common craving to remain emotionally charged "myth-believing" children.

CONTENTS

METAPHORS -- LIAISONS & LOVES

METAPHORS OF ICELAND

MISCELLANEOUS METAPHORS

NUMINOUS MIRRORS II

In this –
the second small volume of poetry ---*NUMINOUS MIRRORS*—
I have endeavored to poetically "eclecticize" a variety of themes
remembering always: *'Poetry is a metaphorical art, which
Science could, but chooses to leave un-explicated'.*

#1
Curiosity is the engine that drives NUMINOUS awakening as
well as the human quest for 'reaching' to what are sometimes
called higher states of consciousness. Being curious means
we will seek and enjoy a state of awesome, ever-unfolding
awareness. Notwithstanding the quest to awaken and reach for
higher consciousness each time we conjure some emotional
REFLECTION or blame other people or outside circumstances
we give a bit of our personal awakening away.

The metaphors of poetry frequently facilitate awakening
because poetry often forces us to see multiple meanings within
the same word/metaphor construct.

A corollary would teach us that blame, rage, or yelling, quashes
our own progress toward "awakening." Please note the use of
aware, awake, higher consciousness and personal power can
be interchangeable.

Being authentically spiritually awake embraces the
understanding that (1) We are never victims of any person
or environmental situation. (2) We actively experience and
interpret our reality. (3) We are responsible for our personal
emotions, perceptions, and interpretations. Why? Because:
Our human brain is constantly perusing, sensing, perceiving,
and then interpreting every experience. Therefore, in a very
literal sense, poetry requires cerebral interpretation – or one

could say human brain function, particularly our emotional responses, force us to create our own reality!

Blaming or accusing others is like having a nighttime dream and then, in our dreams, blaming another person for hurting our 'dream feelings'. Think about it … in our dreams, there is no 'other person' – it is just our brain pretending to be someone else. Just as it is silly to blame someone in our dreams for a hurt feeling.

It is just as silly to blame someone in our everyday lives for hurting our feelings. (This is why religious 'blasphemy' is so obviously laughable.)

#2
During our usual or ordinary states of awareness, it sometimes appears that our <u>emotions are compelling</u> us to act in a certain way. When such compelling occurs, It seems our personal perception of reality diminishes or even departs altogether. We may angrily re-act with assumed motives of 'positive reclamation'—but—when emotions such as anger or frustration manifest, they may also be seen as an attempt to reclaim bits of numinous awakening we have already given away. This is an all too common human misstep – and reeks of misplaced regret. Some of the poems within reflect this kind of loss.

Anger, frustration, jealousy, or any reactive emotion, usually emerges as an effort to vacate our own reasonability—which may take the form of a feeling of loss. We sometimes give our personal power away via expression of emotions (e.g. catharsis) that are the result of believing that someone or some external force has taken something from us, <u>or</u> perhaps more importantly, possesses something we need.

#3

What does it look like to re-take <u>ownership</u> of our personal power or our mental perceptions? I want to be really clear here: As we 'wake' to numinous reflections we realize that we are interpreting or projecting our personal reality (I.E. our perception). When we own our perceptions -- projections and emotions -- we take responsibility for everything in our experience; this includes all that happens in life, as well as everything of which we are conscious. If we are aware of something, even if it is just a so-called 'bad' word, it is happening within our aware judgment and therefore it is an expression of our personal sensory interpretation. Nothing is happening outside of us without our added take or personally constructed cerebral analysis.

When we pass judgment on ourselves for perceiving life's negative disharmony, we actually create more emotional disharmonies. Instead of repeated self-blame, or creating a separate world into which rational thought eludes us, it is rather a matter of finding the parallel perception in our own experience, and reallocating it. When we discover that the disharmony is in ourselves we can harmonize it.

And finally, here's one of the real bottom-bottom lines: taking responsibility can only be accomplished without self-judgment, self-blame or self-criticism. It really is a matter of survival by self-care. Love yourself first! <u>YES – we must first put on our own oxygen mask before we can be of service to anyone else!</u>

Finally, when we are emotionally awake, there is <u>nothing</u> <u>'out there'</u> to which to react – if we don't like what is going on in our interior 'out there perception' of reality, we find the corresponding cause, which is always inside ourselves and we then realign our thoughts, beliefs, emotions, and actions. This is a positive way to *make lemonade*.

Being responsible for our own reality does not automatically make us "Magicians of manifestation" or even more importantly make us responsible for another's emotional interpretation of their reality! The tricky part is being responsible for our experience and interpretation of reality. You may choose to see lemon juice as lemonade but it is not a _new_ objective "manifest reality".

This means that when our friends are having a taxing experience, we don't take responsibility for their emotional experience and attempt to "un-tax" it. We allow them to have their own interpretation of their reality, without trying to control them or change IT or name them "poor little thing", as if you are responsible for their emotional experience. More often than not, your endeavor to "un-tax" will only enable.

Once we 're—member' to be here NOW and understand that our emotionally driven understanding of the outside world is our perception via our senses -- we have unlimited authority to change ourselves, particularly our emotional state, hence change our perception of the world.

The real secrets: (1) 'Life itself is the proper binge' because 'Life is change, life is progress, life is evolving' ... (2) when we attempt to describe our perceptions we typically use what is called metaphor, and all of us can be metaphorically connected via language. (3) "It just doesn't matter!" – Ultimately because "An open mind is not an empty mind"

METAPHORS of SCIENCE

Actually, words cannot help but "lie." Science is the only way that we human beings have found to accurately communicate with each other -- across the boundaries of language and cultures -- without misunderstanding (ie lies) -- because science requires repetition and constructed, consensually validated evidence before it can be considered as a 'possible fact' to be disseminated via communication. Saying "Science is like another belief system" is tantamount to saying "abstinence is another sexual position".

Tribute to Schrödinger ... His paradoxical thought experiment was proposed in 1935.

A cat is placed in a steel box along with a Geiger counter, a vial of poison gas, a hammer, and a radioactive substance. When the radioactive substance decays, the Geiger detects it and triggers the hammer to release the poison gas, which subsequently kills the cat.

The radioactive decay is a random process, and there is no way to predict when it will happen. Physicists say the atom exists in a state known as a superposition—both decayed and not decayed at the same time.

 Until the box is opened, an observer has no way of knowing whether the cat is alive or dead—because the cat's fate is intrinsically tied to whether or not the atom has decayed. The cat would, as Schrödinger put it, be "living and dead ... in equal parts of probability" until it is observed.

CAT IN THE BOX

To sum up --
The famous physics paradox
A Cat, perhaps belonging
To none other
Than Dr. Schrodinger
Himself

We can't see him
Or his cat in the box
Logically and in reality
We can't see if "it" is dead or alive
Probably why he famously thought up
allegedly thoughtful thought experiment

Thus one cannot now tell which path of
probability has now become reality
until we now know - we know - since we cannot now know
he said we must now assume both:
Living & Dead
Thus the insatiable paradox
Now knowing is theoretical -- ironically absurd

Living or dead?
Reality... or ?
Depends on how we choose to see things
Literal or theoretical? Assume both?
Herein lies the puzzle
Wave and particle -- one or the other?

Then too--
As I savor & walk among majestic
Redwood monarchs of Northern California
A cluster of animated college students
arrives suddenly
creating vibrant circles of excitement
making a most colossal cinch.
embracing a massive tree girth
a girl howls
"It's definitely 4:20!"
Another yells back
"No! It's only a little after 4."
others join announcing different times
at or around 4:20.

Now - You & I know that 4:20 is a time
typical Northern California kids met
to smoke
to get to glazier grassy 'high times'
You & I now know
various times shouted
had no acquaintance to wrist-watches.
no bond – no interact – no, not an iota
of anciently
understood
clock time,
sand time or
sundial sequences.

Kid's cluster was relating comparisons of *how high they felt.*
Indeed… all theoretical ie
the now & how we "capture"
TIME
Or SPACE
or the living & dead
cat –

Quantum Theory not for naive wanna-be's!
Contingent on/in what/how
we are thoughtfully educated
to see "things"
L i t e rally –
OR
T h e o retically –
OR
P a r a doxically
OR --?

A study of 30,000 subjects sought to examine the relationship between stress and the perception that stress affects health and mortality.

Both higher levels of reported stress and the perception that stress affects health were independently associated with an increased likelihood of worse health and mortality.

High amounts of stress and the perception that stress impacts health are each associated with poor health and poor mental health. Individuals who perceived that stress affects their health and reported a large amount of stress had an increased risk of premature death.

STRESS

Stress – when seen as negative
  becomes human's nemesis
    causes bio/neurological damage
    myriads of health risks as well
    stress - stressful because
      sapiens perceive it so?

  Some thousands interrogated
    how much stress endured?
      acknowledged high stress --- Bad!
      Stats show increased risk of death.
        Yes, "death is -- ultimate stressor"
          But only those who <u>believed </u>it so!

Others acknowledged high level of stress ---
  Yet had <u>lowest risk of poor health or dying</u>
    stress : blood vessels constrict
      heart rate increases.
        change your mind about stress,
          change your body's response to stress.

    One group told "pounding heart gears for action,
      Increased breathing brings beneficial brain oxygen"
        Result: viewed stress as helpful
          less anxious - more confident.
            blood vessels stayed relaxed
              cardiovascular reactions mirrored joy.

No one is impervious to stress.
  not whether we experience stress;
    it's how we respond.
      Placebo – anyone?

Nature (2010) reported marine Phytoplankton have declined in the world's oceans over the past century. Phytoplankton concentrations in surface waters were estimated to have decreased by about 40% since 1950 alone -- most probably in response to global warming. The study generated debate among scientists and several criticisms were also published in _Nature_.

Phytoplankton are vital components of the ocean's ecological community and a key factor of all seas and freshwater basin ecosystems. The name comes from the _Greek_ words φυτόν (phyton), meaning, "plant", and πλαγκτός (planktos), meaning "wanderer" or "drifter". Too small to be seen with the unaided eye phytoplankton, when present in high enough numbers, may appear as green discoloration of the water due to the presence of chlorophyll within their cell walls.

GAIA'S LIFE CYCLE

Desert Sands secrete & hoard humid dampness
While seas of blue/green boast bountiful wetness
our Oceans create moist heat to cremate dust
sent to unknown parts of Terra's sandy crust
myriads of bleak dry bites of mites and gusts
remain damp with living reservoirs unseen
microscopic animals blown to smithereens
soggy wind swirls and living dust-devils
from desert sands to shimmering sea
launch life from multi-levels to be free

Phytoplankton, single-celled sea plants
Firmly fix their tiny moist jade digit tat
to tightly rule Gaia's desert thermostat!
As Sol's photons shine brightly –
plankton plants grow abundantly
allow departing heat to rise hastily
producing soggy *dimethyl-sulphide*
DMS delivers profusions of petite plants
Gaia's green-house/arid air by chance
seed life-nourishing nascent cloud kin
conveying life-giving rain to breathe
Gaia's thriving marine cover water skin

Dark clouds form and abruptly grow
hence hinder Gaia's newly heated temperature
opaque gas haze obstructs *plankton rapture*
essential sunlight diffuses - weakens cell verdure…
slow growth - fewer clouds form - reheat dissipate.
Notwithstanding -- cycles continue to perpetuate
the living globe! Her self-regulation persists
dare WE despoil Gaia's wet ocean womb
garbage, glass, trash & lethal drivel – must desist *

Phytoplankton controls
the creation of our clouds
our lenient temperatures
imperative for profligate *homo sapiens*-
notwithstanding -- living mechanisms bear time's test
maniac human organisms lack
never think how haughty creatures attack & <u>interact</u>
& relentlessly spoil & sack symbiotic Gaia-
except living - now dying – spaceship planet ransacked

*Anyone doubting human involvement in 'global warming' need only look at how
we have despoiled our oceans ---

Marie Curie was nominated for a French honor, became a French hero when she received a foreign tribute -- two Nobel Prizes.

In 1911 it was revealed that in 1910–11 Curie had conducted an affair of about a year's duration with physicist Paul Langevin, a former student of Pierre's—a married man who was estranged from his wife. This resulted in a scandal that was exploited by her academic opponents. Curie (then in her mid-40s) was five years older than Langevin and was misrepresented in the tabloids as a foreign Jewish home-wrecker. When the scandal broke, she was away at a conference in Belgium; on her return, she found an angry mob in front of her house and had to seek refuge, with her daughters, in the home of a friend.

The fickle hypocritical "public" has long been silenced but the fact that the Royal Swedish Academy of Sciences, overcoming opposition prompted by the affair scandal, honored her a second time, with the 1911 Nobel Prize in Chemistry. This award was "in recognition of her services to the advancement of chemistry by the discovery of the elements radium and polonium, by the isolation of radium and the study of the nature and compounds of this remarkable element." She was the first and only woman to receive two Nobel Prizes.

LIGHT FROM ROCK

Gullible Marie Curie - et al - had
ideas curious - credulous and bad
as bidden & forbidden Eden's sad dyad
together as one - then two - they unearthed
exposed & posed rocks that talk & mock
beheld in burnt offering atoms' divine death
exposed naked in benign baroque rock
lethal impasse - a nip of gridlock deadlock
dirty reductions of nascent pitchblende stone
unheralded death -- Radium fiercely shown

In glowing radiance yet silent luminosity
she embraced the perilous monstrosity
in gullible hands without shields of lead
Curie naïvely pondered and misread
the invisible smirks that stole her life
and joined her soul to a lethal source
A radiant authority to which she forced
& dedicated her life to loss instead

Not deterred by what alchemists told
that magic morphed lead to gold
sans God's divinely flawed retort
spuriously she saw its matrix fall short
painstakingly the sacred pinch of demise
was (and is) a benign dust atomized
from God's benign creation -- lies materialized

Our ever-growing glowing myths comprise
Pandora's box creaked opened & raised
deadly demise a Nobel Prize legitimized
Too late her ignominious end was realized
the jeopardous glowing quixotic gem chastised
forbidden fire slow obliteration now symbolized
lustrous glow also harbored a fatal death knell
as Chiron rows his lethal raft athwart Styx to Hell

Death's radiance evoked the pulsating light
continued publishing inglorious purposes
birthing headlines for galaxies & fading sight
barely discernable quasars at night
reveal bits of creation's death-ray light
a primeval Big Bang fireballs seem to mock
life & death creations from simple rock
morbid matter & energy now once more done
Life & death known & seen at once as one

Yes, we can actually 'watch' the evolution of viruses and some other micro-bugs. But for the ever-shrinking group of religionists -- Evolution is evil - because it demands we consider Science, rather than musty, mostly conjured myths, as explanatory.

However many still assert that arrogant Homo sapiens are the end-to-end all! What they call "dominion over" and provide "holy images and ideas" that refuse to evolve. To what end? Space and what is now called 'dark matter' are both alive with ever-evolving data,

MYSTERY SOLVED

What is this thing called 'Cosmos'?
       From whence to where?
What is this mania to dub a mystery?
       From whom -- to whom?
Some name delusions & illusions 'Faith'
       Peek as they boogie and bop

Quietly shake our heads in bafflement
       From now 'til a future puzzlement
On and in the alleged cosmic supposition
       From guess and speculation
We discern and label it black vacant vacuous
       Yet science sees astonishing texture

The vacuous gap's not bare or blank or barren
       IT Reeks of Higgs boson mass
Then collides in weighted building blocks
       fills the Mathematical dreams
of beautiful minds and lends measured heaviness
       to form creation itself: LOGOS --

We in ever-growing hubris must assert and declare
        human importance in our prideful repertoire
Thus we call "self" as vital for viewing spirit spectacular
        While life's dark space morphs -- not bare
Are the *Sapiens* empty and arrogantly vacant yet dare
        Heavy-handed imaginés thrust everywhere?

Is quantum physics the smallest of the small?
        Vibe or particle - What do we fail to call?
Answer: A question that asks a question Is not a question! *
        Yet the "thing" changes by mere observation
Or did one such being assert a truth as while he bawled
        And repeated –- what may not be --- at all?

* (Neil dG Tyson)

It also considers that the mind and body are separate; the body consists of ordinary matter and the mind in some way differs from this. This leads one to speculate as to how they differ. In explaining this, the philosopher Rene Descartes (1596-1650) was prominent. His influence was such that we still speak of Cartesian Dualism. His idea? Primarily that mind and brain were separate. His work was sanctioned by the popular church adding to the acceptability of his theory. Descartes utilized human anatomy itself in his explanation. For him, the pineal gland was the locus where body and mind connected. Today we know the pineal gland is responsible for producing melatonin, which responds to light levels and hence was often considered a '3rd eye'. (In metaphysics this third eye is responsible for intuitive and psychic abilities!) However, Descartes reasoned that it was a single gland and that only occurred in the human species therefore, it was the connecting spot for the mind and body—The soul's abode?

Mechanistic Descartes reasoned that a sensory nerve (e.g., optic nerve) was like a tube through which 'vital spirits' flowed, this sent messages to the ventricles in the brain, animal spirits would then flow back through the nerves to muscles in the body.

Still, Cartesian theory helped to lay the foundations for the modern development of the scientific study of the brain.

Magnetic Resonance (fMRI) research has pretty well shown that the brain and body function as a whole rather than as two or more distinct parts.

DUALISM

No duplicity exists in our world of natural oneness
It is born from emotional human thought
"Reverend's" power-seeking creates dualism
Genesis Believers construct "good" - "evil"
Eden's problems polarized by split thought

Division makes possible Cantors & Cardinals
emotional conflict-ridden cerebral endowment
creates religious Priesthood deities then deifies
impure *Bast-Pashti Goddesses* & profane Gods
Divisive -- respectable & rude -- holy and unholy

Imams & Ayatollahs create claims
Of Devil and God dualities partition
Heavenly idol clones & hell's twin
Fictitious rights and wrongs
Dominance of Men over Women

Twofold states of mystical worlds
Do not thrive in innate natural nature
It is only the emotional *Sapiens* mind
That subdues, conquers & fractals
the oneness of a factual cohesive world

Shaman's wet cortices' tear asunder Gaia's unity
Claim to visit via drugged brain, mystical other world
Ascribe evil to the magnificent eagles & condors
When they return bloody flesh to a hungry nest –
Majestic flights-symbolic? Or evolutionary survival?

Bast, Bbhikkhus & Bishops crush the mono-natural
Arriving at a dualist world made safe for terrorists
Belief in dualisms allows emotion driven believers
to condone slaughter of "the other" the "not me"
Does propitiating Bodhisattvas really aid enlightenment?

Whenever I hear someone quote some esoteric Quantum research – <u>as if</u> they actually know the profound mathematics or physical science behind the statement - I am perplexed. Until one has studied Physics for at least ten years and then taken advanced degrees in math and algorithms ... Please don't try to impress me or anyone with your interpretive version - because you really don't have any idea what you are talking about!

QUIXOTE -- THE QUANTUM MECHANIC

Man from La Mancha (saw it in NT 50 years ago.)
Had tears then -- and again -- identifying with Don Quixote
pulling on Knight's accoutrements --- charging inanely forth
insanely jousting with windmills - delusion appears authentic
Yet, no real relationship present. Life's an illusion.
We linger for Sancho - detest Panza
decipher that -- oh wise ones

Quantum Physicists may espouse "no human fantasy" –
no matter how improbable -- is impossible.
typewriter monkeys, given infinite amounts of time,
could replicate Bible -- disciples of New Age hyperbole
utilize physics -- particularly Q physics,
proving within their pompous mind cavities
fascinating -- unsupportable presumptions

When fantasizing about the possible
it is again always well to repeatedly affirm:
Possible is miles away from
Probable -- and as scientific method demonstrates
Bankable is miles away from Probable.
Correlation is never defined as *Causation*
Our illusions are placed in mysterious misty mists

Agreeing with undeniable researchers,
rational, skeptical, incredulous (& cynical?)
yet arrogant *homo sapiens* insist
believing soul, spirit, or consciousness
life "going on" after one's demise.
promised immortality is a rosy ruse.
particular particles probably will "go on."

There it is again: "probable"
vibration rhythms will continue—
even if bacterial or viral in nature.
it may well be that our true purpose:
life forms -- microbes, bugs. viruses
living in and on you and me
in the uncounted billions will survive.

Again with every newly acquired theory,
arrogant *Homo sapiens* fancy for eternal life
in one form or another is announced
lied about then tied around some misconstrued
so called Q for quixotic subjective brainchild.
Our Quixote announces the ultimate hubris creation:
"God made in his own image." HA! Panza!

Never in a million years did I think I would still have access to the column pedestal my father built nearly fifty years ago to hold my lecture notes when I was teaching at the University. Yet here it is, only now it holds a massive unabridged dictionary, This holy tome is born of systematic rational logic rather than myth and the hocus pocus of make-believe stories. Verified, logic and rational "word-smithing" is what makes a book sacred.

FINDING TRUE KNOWLEDGE

Years ago I read at the big book
--The Unabridged Dictionary --
Hoping against hope to find
secret meanings
Con-
joined words or
ink-
lings of magic and mystery
These were special words
not arbitrary scrawls
on a telephone pad
done unconsciously
while thought traveled
at warp speed
elsewhere

Unknown
and
unmentionable, unfathomable
mind seas could be explored
with Dictionary word buoys
like enchanted carbon corks
used to copy squiggled spells,
potions & philters
that float by to astonish
inquisitive sailors &
curious book lovers
with the charm
of their freshly
scrutinized
buoyancy

My frequent journeys
to the massive unabridged
tome resting open,
at ease,
on a hand-made pillar
(Grecian Doric lectern)
was most times
a dopamine epiphany of pleasure
Oozing
from ever fecund contagion
of reflective thought troves
that made known
literal power over things
by conjuring
other abstruse
words
like "hocus-pocus" and "sesame"
Before APP spelling programs
usurped
our cryptic cerebral requests
we took ownership of our own memory chips
for reality spelling – rather than 'spells'
the children
who knew
'dictionary use'
knew :
1. to distinguish
fact from fantasy
2. myths, miracles, and fairy tales
now found lodging -- not in fact
but in *Fiction's* book-stack
section

in my mind,
not Lego's
but reading at the colossal tome
held my attention for hours
meanings and enchantment merged
the way a single word
possesses power over things
nouns, verbs and adjectives
like some esoteric ancient relic collection
gathered thoughts
correlated letters
as Cabala numbers
are said to explain relationship
between Jehovah and Man
Jewish mysticism and meditation
words in that vast word work contained
some surreptitious
secrets revealed
not hidden for only a few
Ahs!

The organized progression!
The mathematic-like precision!
The detailed alphabetical order!
Magic' is - in due course - followed
by 'mysterious' & then 'myth'
such rational logic left no one
mythologized
baffled
by woo woo

Human emphasis on eyesight or insight is often overstated. It is <u>not</u> the eye that sees—especially the so-called "third eye." Sight has little to do with the lens we call eye and everything to do with the human brain.

EYE SIGHT & WORD MEANING

not the eye
but the mind
sees!
our Interpreting brain
inures
insures mysteries
abide because
within newer technology
eyeballs are superfluous
to signs, words and thought
like gushing water to the rainbow
photons of light are essential
revelatory of prism multi colors
digitized molecules are essential
rather than eyeball itself

ink lettered
mole
cules
morph
to
word symbols
fin
ally
a
thought

Through the thin liquid wall
separating world of things
from the world of mind
Inchoate digital light blobs
assault vitreous lens
        then retina
        then optic nerve tube
becoming defined things of thought
only when digitized light atoms
alight via synapses
on the hind brain lobe
where only then
sapiens' mind
begins the
mystery of
interpretations

Have you ever wondered why both political and religious conversations were considered 'anathema' at quixotic, tasteful dinner parties? Have you ever considered the content of successful discussions between different people, especially where conversation and explication led to solutions?—Only rarely does someone accept new 'Now' empirical data and actually change a long-held point of view. How rare! Why? The human brain uses emotion as a great trickster and most want to remain innocent as an emotionally charged child.

BELIEF or BELIE?

Yes solutions do happen
They present themselves!
As if ether-gods are clappin'
regard or discard?

Existing in 'mind's intuition'
Emotionally charged beliefs
When threatened by elucidation
buffed or rebuffed?

Disquieted bright people also believe
'Now'-data then defy defied belief
facts vanquish myth & grief
recognize or snub?

Show brainy Democrat Stat:
"guns slash home invasion crime"
Invasion now morphs to non-issue
say yes or deny?

Black or White solutions
harvests of human belief
not divine plant or conclusion
'bona fide' or 'belie'

Professor Whorf

viewed language (words) as the determiner of what the individual brain perceives in this world and how he/she thinks about it. These word patterns vary widely, thus the thinking and perceiving by peoples utilizing different language systems will result in basically different worldviews. "The same physical perceptual evidence does not lead observers to the same perception, unless their linguistic backgrounds are similar..."

For example, in the Indo-European languages, words (adjectives and verbs) appear as basic grammatical units. So that, for example, Inuit peoples perceive at least twenty types of snow and have words that describe each.

Another of Whorf's arguments was the difference in the understanding of time as a conceptual category among the Hopi. He argued that in contrast to English, the Hopi language does not treat the flow of time as a sequence of distinct, countable instances, like "three days" or "five years," but rather as a single process. Therefore since their language does not have nouns referring to units of time, he proposed that their view of time explained certain Hopi behavioral patterns related to punctuality etc.

WD40 PROPAGANDA

Willingly we accept myths-
the shiny ancient tales of
glossy propaganda
even as empirical evidence
advocates human brain itself
more than adequate
explaining "extra-usual"
perceptions

Willingly in times past
slick folklore
attributed to souls
spirits or sly
other-world essence –
expressed black and white
silky smooth oily propaganda
received as new naked "truth"

Willingly now define spiritual
as awe - wonder – amazement
subjective numinous expressions
in open upended unending surprise
filling multi luxurious legends
exaggerated like life itself –
we cheerlead for the inscrutable
longing for more a-ha experiences

Willingly our life mirror has not two –
but myriads of sides
-apprehended epiphanies rare,
-slick propaganda common
no realistic stopping point
never one or even a
two sided
truth emerges

Willingly Dr. Whorf offers
a scrap of possibility:
language -- words themselves
create our preconceived reality's
overblown lubricated propaganda
words turn mind into prisons of thought
like Eskimos' twenty snow avowals
proclaim propaganda - & it propagates

A new survey by anthropologists calls into question the scientific and historic justification for the popular 'Paleo diet'. Early man/woman, these researchers say, was an opportunist, not a nutritionist or dieter. The trendy diet is named for the Paleolithic Age, (the epoch of prehistory characterized by so-called cavemen and primitive stone tools.) Today's sincere Paleo dieters forgo grains and processed foods in favor of meat, fish, and vegetables.

The emphasis of protein and whole foods isn't without merit, but its genesis is based on the idea that humans were at their physical and nutritional best some 10 thousand to 2.5 million years ago -- before the modern diet was corrupted by the advent of agriculture—particularly Genetically Modified wheat.

However, there is little confirmation that early hominids had specialized diets or specific food categories that seemed particularly imperative. Researchers say early <u>Homo-Sapiens</u> ate based on survivability and availability. The percentage of protein incorporated in the diets of Paleolithic peoples varied from place to place, depending on climate and geology. Furthermore: today's meats, fruits and vegetables are entirely different than the types of things people were finding in the fields and forests thousands/(millions?) of years ago.

Most researchers agree - assuming Paleo peoples were healthier than modern man is ill advised. Paleolithic people had short life spans, never living long enough to become susceptible to diseases like cancer and other so-called diseases of "old age" or modern dietary influences. Throughout the majority of human evolutionary history, balancing the diet was not a big issue. They were simply in survival mode-- acquiring enough calories to survive and reproduce.

PALEO WOMAN

Ancient Paleo Woman did it all
Enhanced her cave clan via health-food
  vicious delicious eatable victuals
    Paleo woman -- alleged
     Stronger - hardier
     Leaner - tougher
      improved - Systems
      Superior - immunity

Ancient Paleo women ate it all
Imprinted her clan's DNA
  For five million years
  Wild food
   Wild game
    Wild greens
    Wild fruits
    Wild bugs

Just a few thousand years ago
Modern homo horror began:
  Agriculture
  GM Wheat
   Germ resistant grains
    Spray poisons
     Chemicals Fertilize

Early Hominids
Abandoned basic-x
  Subsequent diet
    has new relevance
      For understanding
        Present day weaknesses
          Infesting humanoids
          And life itself

Insectivores require one of the
most excellent things on this planet
      For humanoid nutrition
        Bug-protein supplied by Paleo women
          grew our brains and our bodies
            via available sustainable obtainable
              Nutritional creepy bugs & insects
                in support of *Sapiens* omnivores
                new large brain size

'Homo erectus' changed
Morphed inside & outside
   advantage: *Homo Sapiens*
    spiritual ability to be curious
      seek variety of sources.
        Occam-razor-sharp Paleo woman
          moved (ran) to Savannah
            saw both prey & predators
              as they acquired upright stance

ingesting enough vegetable matter
took time to balance vegan diets
   BUT as time and digging
   would and does tell
    these newer versions of
    ultimate *Homo sapiens*
    ate any and all protein
     insect versions
      supplied by Paleo women

Neither New World apes or old world
Hominids: chimpanzees & gorillas,
   (neither Neanderthals nor Cro-Magnon)
   avoided this higher quality woman food -
   namely an appetite for creepy crawlies
    concentrated ideal nutrient sources
     in themselves as abundant
      as leafs, fruits, flowers and even nuts.

Bugs eat bugs - and other crawling insects
The clever Paleo woman knew
  thereby concentrating within
   their own spindly legs & tissues
    nutrients found in multi-myriad plant sources
     providing sorts of protein their clan and
      morphing primate babes needed
       high calories – fresh organic health
       plus best of all essential fatty acids.

Insects - scrumptious compact packages -
that allowed *sapiens* in her care
  fresh proteins to survive and thrive
  human digestive process much easier -
  energy no longer mislaid or expended
   by foraging ancestors gathering nutrition.
   nutrients condensed in bugs concentrated

Termites and tools required to forage them
attracted much attention last century
  termites helpful source of protein fat & amino acids.
   rump steak yields 322 calories per hundred grams
    termites provide 560 calories per hundred grams
     evolving proto human must choose
      termites source of protein - no required running
      or precisely thrown rock or lance
      or a 2 minute breath-hold down 20 feet.

Insect eating is a drive-through window
at the survivable Cosmic "Inner/Outer".
  big caloric payoffs for low energy output.
   Yes, early Paleo women were skillful hunters --
    bringing home meat much of the time.
     brutish men were rarely triumphant
     often returned empty-handed
     to cave and clan

whereas Paleo woman stayed near home
and sought at least some creepy thing
to feed her ravenous families
and most importantly - surviving kids.
their proteins consisted of insects.
Paleo female saw a big bug
and shrieked, screamed in
ecstasy & exhilaration

Yes our times have changed!
Even knowing lunch is obtainable
for her family currently easily available*
modern *wisdom filled women*
scream in fear and flee the
crucial vital insect victuals
and her new *Homo sapiens*
now lack essential nutrition

* science suggests we are never more than 6 ft away from a spider

Notwithstanding the hype- you don't actually control your thoughts. Thoughts appear to come and go as they please, without any regard as to whether you want them to or not. The answer to the question-- "How can I prevail over thoughts that enter my mind during meditation" -- is simple - you can't!

However, as always, there is a practical, Occam's razor, solution to most human problems in life. You may not be able to control thoughts that come into your mind, but you can control how long they stay and the impact they have.

The secret many meditating Yogis will share is: "Your mind will usually naturally find equilibrium after 20 minutes."

What that means is: that if you can gradually train yourself to sit quietly for 20 minutes (simply observing your thoughts and breath,) your mind will automatically slow and the number of thoughts entering without you having to do anything will automatically diminish. To ensure ongoing equilibrium or homeostasis- Life requires balance! If you do not attempt to practice it ... life will find a way ... even via death itself – the ultimate homeostasis.

NOT SO SILENT MEDITATIONS

Everything I have been
Everything I am now
Everything is possible
my future is here now

Since anticipation's future
also fashions my identity
in the transitory present
Meditation is today's now

My meditations
are never only one thing
Among my meditations are
voiceless multi-conversations

In silent artful meditations:
I try listening to myself
I shout hopeful stuff
I didn't know I knew

But *Hope* is an illusion
Try is a deceptive chimera
I Hope for courage
I Try to act courageously

I Hope for a daring way
To express thanks to another
Without having my heart broken
This too is an illusion

French *Coeur* means Heart
In my heartfelt meditations
I hope for ways to be courageous
without crushing the *Coeur of others*

There is no friend,
who won't break your heart.
your mission will find you wanting.
Examine your own integrity,

To be human without heartbreak
Is not possible in this life
so why not get on with it?
Stop wanting heartlessness!

For as long as I can remember, it has occurred to me that to believe in myths and gods and then arrogantly insist that children be indoctrinated with such things - then contend that the child's mind accept such as absolute truth - could be ultimately confusing. Sure enough, recent research has shown that when 5 & 6 year olds have been indoctrinated with religious doctrine and mythology they have difficulty differentiating Fact from Fiction.

GIVING ADVICE

To "go into all the world"
  To give advice to another
  To condescendingly presume
    To point another to reputed ideal
      Thus insuring their eventual "eternity"
      Is/As their ultimate ambition

Only a conceited fool would dare
 Advocate such arrogant egomania
   Children duped by ideologue myths
   Of the Big Three religion teachers
   Cognitive Scientist researchers
     Discern 5 & 6 year olds have difficulty
     Differentiating Fact from Fiction
       Teaching or abusing - is the question
       Lies and mythology
       Sanity or insanity?

Gallop Polls report majority of *sapiens*
 Still, in the land of the free
    Believe -- yes -- holy Bible damns–
    Not Slavery,
      but homosexuality,
       and masturbation
       and equality for women
         For fixed believers and bible advocates –
Such sins worthy of eternal damnation
as word of God declares Bible truth
Literal truth by true believers ... true?
  Yet there may be venues available
   for giving and taking advice:

Maybe it is possible --TO --

Be just a little kinder
Learn the value of what we call 'time'.
Find success in perseverance.
Appreciate the pleasure of labor
Rather than I-phone blather
Acknowledge the worth of honesty--
And again --The power of kindness.
And forgiveness, especially of self
As well as the influence of example.
And the wisdom of Occam's razor

Breathe in the early morning -- noon beginnings are too late
Love's a word oft too easy --
Yes -- Use the word -- and mean it!
Stop! You've had enough -- (anti-clean plate club)

BE every day ever curious
    Accept the rush of new information
        Rather than hashing rehashing
            The scuttle of old anecdotes
                There is more 'magic' revealed
                    By YouTube, Vertasium, TED talks
                than all previous centuries
Science ideas do change and morph
precisely why "science systems"
differ from "belief systems"

                Collect data on causation vs correlation.
                Children love correlations & myths
                some adults never choose
                to be "born again" as adults.
I wonder …
is belief in myths –
an attempt to remain uninformed
thus 'innocent & blameless' child?

Many world Analysts say that Islam is by far the gravest religious threat to the world at large because of its "comfort with violence" (e.g. Contrary to PC hype, the core of 9/11 was religious -- not cultural, political, or economic.) Note: the majority of the Muslim world cheered when the NY towers went down. The largest part of the mayhem in today's world is rooted in a thousand years of Muslim religious hatred and conflict- literally and specifically: 1) Dismissal of half of their population (female gender as being inferior) based on Jewish & Muslim male readers and interpreters of ancient sacred literature (2) The ancient rift between Sunni and Shia. (3) The degeneration of American Christianity into the crudest forms of paranoia (fundamentalism).

Nonsense, like psychosis, is that which when examined in the cool light of day, will be seen to "not make logical sense" (i.e. repeating the same, identical activity while still expecting a different outcome).

ISIS: SISSY SISTER

The mortar's open mouths
  Gobble incendiary rounds
    Pumped unmercifully to towns
    Already blown by drones

In an infinite instant nano-sec
  A desert sky goes gray with fleck
    The roaring avalanche of bombs
      Crushes life from clay-brick homes

God & Goddess of 'non-religious' war
  Looks with smiling satisfaction
    And stridently insist on still more
      Of promised pseudo paradise reaction

Yes, Isis kids imitate ersatz sounds
  of USA's sick pseudo war world 'round
    dying for religious clowns posing
    offering smiles whilst decomposing

examine Boko Haram bizarre upheaval
  brutish bullies—hormones? or teenage evil
    lying in the name of the god Allah -- typical
      Because "be_lie_f" & "_whor_ship" are identical

America has rapidly become the most obese country in the world. We have diets and programs without end – and addictions. America's addiction to food tops the list. Resent research suggests that perhaps it is not the brain craving for food but rather the lack, in most Americans, for social contact and intimacy. With our growing dependence on the Internet as well as isolating forms of transportation and quick foods (where we typically gobble without speaking) isolation becomes endemic and a way-of-life,

The isolation problem grows exponentially in our prison system and will continue to grow despite our 'band aide' treatment plans. We need to learn the discipline of how to create social interaction.

Discipline comes from the same root word as disciple, which has nothing to do with suffering and pain. Rather, its root meaning is to pursue and learn. Perhaps it is time to begin to pursue and discover anew the basic benefits of social interaction --

Without which -- addiction is birthed.

OBESITY

My personal problem with obesity:
My need of discipline in my life –
My personal lack - my failure
Obese persons 'represent'
And remind me
MY lack of discipline
My fear of others
My problem not theirs!

If every day I am ever curious
Accepting and talk to new friends
about rush of new information.
But rather than the exercise
of new thought and change
I hash rehash the trash
of the scuttle of old anecdotes
I grow obese with inaction

Rather, let's talk about the 'magic'
revealed by, NOVA or TED talks-
than all previous myths & sacred texts.
Science ideas do change and morph
precisely why 'science systems'
differ from 'belief systems'
Separate causation from correlation.

Children love correlations & fictional stories
It appears that some adults never choose
to grow up as sociable, thinking adults.
I wonder …
"is belief in myths – and fixed thought
an attempt to remain a chubby child?"

METAPHORS of PALM SPRINGS

When I moved to "Palm Springs" a few years ago--strictly an effort to recapture the stable texture and unwavering warmth of Hawaii where I had lived for decades and by my old rationale: "Live in a tourist zone – 'they' already know the most ideal places in the world!" – I found I had had to modify my thinking.

Far from stability and constant temperature I found more variability than I had imagined.

Besides wonderful winter climate and unpredictable freezes, Palm Springs is also renowned for its wealth of plastic surgeons (pun intended).

Surgical clipping and filling are standard procedures for both men and women as they make their pilgrimage to this 'Mecca in the desert' to have their body parts excised or supplemented.
Thus another addiction is birthed in "Sunny land."

A Pantoum is composed of a series of verses; the second and fourth lines are repeated as the first and third lines of the next.

PALM SPRINGS (December 2013)

Snowbirds unpack and don anew coat & muff
Promptly doffing shorts and summer gear
Escaping Sunless climates -- they'd had enough

Pallid bodies in Palm Springs sans Sol - no cheer
Promptly doffing shorts & summer gear
Now must endure Palm Springs wind and cold

Pallid bodies in Palm Springs sans Sol - no cheer
No doubt regretting the farm's been sold
Promptly doffing shorts and summer gear

Escaping sunless climates – they'd had enough
Now must endure Palm Springs wind and cold
Snowbirds unpack and don anew coat and muff

Palm Springs was a choice. The warmth as well as the architecture has its appeal. Flat roofs, glass walls, and outdoor living add to the winter ambience, which appears to charm most occasional visitors.

Summer is another story and worthy of its own Pantoum...

PALM SPRINGS SUMMER (2013)

Slow ing stroll ing in the Palm Spring summer
        snail's pace gasp ing in the stifling hot ness
            I am burn ing but not up

Grasp ing for the memory of noir shade
        snail's pace gasp ing in the stifling hotness
            A memory holds a shadow tenderly

Grasp ing for the memory of noir shade
        I feel its softness amid the firmness
            snail's pace gasp ing in the stifling hot ness

I am burn ing but not up
        A memory holds a shadow tenderly
            Slow ing stroll ing in the Palm Springs summer

The near perfect days, so often experienced in Palm Springs, are even more prominent during certain seasons.

AUTUMN IN PALM SPRINGS -PS- (2014)

PS Autumn no doubt delights the gods of Elysium
Near 'Perfect' quasi blemished by brisk breeze
Yet dust flaws & Cracks do let in the light per diem
essential -- still alive to variations and disease

Winter --- hot then cold -- become ambivalent rivals
Palm Springs desert winter attracts then repels
Sunshine's warmth 'till three -- then PM freeze revival
Contentment vs happiness – exhale then inhale

Spring – the Halcyon goddess bounces & soars
pounces like a lovable kitten ambushing dust mites
zip and zap athwart freshly waxed floors
that moves lightening like as a furtive mouse might

PS Summer's hell contends for masochist record
We breathe fiery sparks of flames as life's discord
Lizard skin commonplace as sunscreen reward
A time non-motion itself becomes an atypical horde

Without cold where is hot? Sans sizzle -- frost?
Within hell's threat comes the dreaded sun holocaust?
Canada keeps desert commerce alive at little cost
Hollywood types mourn weekend affairs - star crossed

Then there are fun, unpredictable days of Autumn when wind or other unexpected weather events add surprise to the daily venue.

PS FALL DAY - CHAOS THEORY

Windy Autumn breathes and leaves
wisps of leaves askew and a-skittle
No heavy anchors here or there
Hugging clingingly to a muddy base
Now sans a single weight
Leaves wind-winched aloft
aweigh in Fall wind to fall
again
leaving frail leaves
viewing new vistas
Organized chaos
Now arranged
marginalized
Classified
systematized
controlled
much like
herding or funneling
feral felines
minus organization or jurisdiction
uncontrolled shambolism
adds pandemonium to Autumn
yet we sigh and admire the failed Fall day
Dying to winters' wanton wish
The unheeded Autumn constant:
Within Chaos abides a cherished Order

Often Palm Springs has a few bitter cold days in the winter. Then there was the winter of '14. It was so mild as to say "there was no winter".

PS SANS WINTER—(2014)

the vibrant morning hushes
as walkers, joggers, and shufflers
silently shift toward coffee
Summer too is shuffling since solstice
arrived sans usual cooler season

seeming eternal summer days
happily salute eastern-state guests
escaping cold winter prisons
of window high piles of snow
brought, they say, by Terra warming

this warm morning has clear sky
and a few cool clouds amplify
season of eternal summer -- they lie
but days remain indifferent - capricious
they do not listen – complaints horrify

"change it might, change it will" (such guile)
days languidly move as if I am a silent chime
they pass in single salient "endless file"
as has been poetically moniker-ed
and silent as the "daughter of time"

This year is different -- leaving no cool
afternoon in the San Jacinto shade
thus far there is no winter this season
to the delight of the eastern visitors
silently, my dog & I shuffle to hot coffee

The overwhelming rainstorm of – '14 was rare but a recurrent enough event to warrant some flood control measures. But human nature being what it is ...

COACHELLA DESERT DELUGE (9-11 2014)

Stepping out
into the bizarre pale pink morning
Watching uncanny mauve mountains
acquire and embrace a breath of light
as if blocking a dark expected storm
once again twice-born
desert valleys gear for chaos
September eleven – a day of infamy
in America -- celebrated elsewhere
by unfettered Arab applause

exceedingly more anticipated
storm drama shied away
leaving something of a vacuum
a strange shock held destiny's recognition
senses sharpened –
awaiting trumpet's doom blast
but no rocks swayed –
no angels materialized
no greeting for raised Messianic masses
hills stood firm –

our World re--fused termination
Eyes fixed then glazed –
horizon's moisture driven clouds
captured fast ascending light
the clouds burst
upon a bone-dry scene
worthy of photo-shopped 'selfies'
except for bulging breath-holding clouds
dry desert roads celebrate
with swiftly rushing waters dragging cars
bobbing like corks nullifying desert passage

Flash-less floods
pouring over the dry surface of sandy beds
left countenances of beautiful bewilderment
like little kids blameless as king Solomon
who know everything
before 'waking up'
they expose innocent brown faces
like sweet-potato-pies waiting a cool down
within the fresh morning breezes
celebrating desert wetness

METAPHORS -- LIAISONS & LOVES

Scientifically, love may be determined or some would say "reduced" to a brain-induced chemical (i.e. oxytocin plus adrenaline.) However the multi-metaphors that attempt to communicate this synergistic life experience are 'legion'.

Nearly every man who has had an extended relationship, knows the futility of controlling 'wandering impious thoughts'. Recent research has suggested the same may be true for women. The fact of the 'eternal triangle' - is well documented. The almost toxic effect of looking and then creating a dialogue with a new attractive 'other' is indeed like partaking of a new drug. Indeed, the 'frog'-- as if by magic -- becomes 'Prince Charming'

In the final analysis 'forgiveness' may be the ultimate human magnetism!

THE ETERNAL TRIANGLE

Married and taken for granted
she spied a mundane frog and "wished"
　　it "just happened" a prince appeared!
　　　a doting toad who listened with
　　　　singular unerring attention to
　　　　　secrets she ne'er before told

She knew and both 'HEs' knew & toasted
a soiled page spoiling a fabled fairytale marriage
ended via indifference and dreary lackluster
　　the newly sighted frog 'prince' endearingly hoisted
　　　heavy wide eye-lash-less lids to muster
　　　　his ample mouth croaking oxytocin love

Spotted dotted modeled damp complexion
exposed his prior randy bawdy blemished liaisons
　　toxic tocin love links -- astray with STDs reflections
　　　muddy, clammy mucky and flecked with stinks
　　　　as the slimy connubial pond from which dung
　　　　　soggy residence he'd sneakily sprung

She accepted, even expected his toady flaws
but his breathtaking damp flicking tongue lit
　　achieved sensualities hitherto fresh unfamiliar
　　　gasps pants triggered groans and moans
　　　　his long slender tool slid by dainty detours
　　　　　in & out slurping his undying rib-bit, rib-bit

Transported to realms of ecstasy's kiss
by a mere lick of his 'princely' toxic skin
    she inhabited her 'delic' dreamy fairy kingdom
        where wishes of connubial sexed bliss
            crammed cramped egos with vanity discuss
                extravagant banquets of cunnilingus

As randy feral critters will fiddle and coax,
the faux prince, was also wont to flick a toady tongue
    and snap up other transient succulent drifting delights
        that floated, swayed, sashayed & succumbed
            to Prince's venial toxic weapon — his faithlessness
                obscured her fevered appetite for his tonguing

Alas — nothing lasts forever (including orgasms)
halcyon sensual climaxes wilted & drooped abruptly
    hibernation time came suddenly for faux frog prince
        brusquely gruffly he merged with soft slime
            the enchanted oxytocin 'prince' revealed a toad
                nay! Rather 'delic' toxins had projected "prince"

He burped a 'rib bit' & turned noxious again
she screamed & squealed a remorseful howl
    her hexed lackluster ex had found another
        yet dreary non-venomous, forlorn and lonely
            he mercifully -- with a poetic gesture forgave her
                She was his - a certain confident contentment

Self-assured he hopped to her side sans 'delic' toxins
a momentous meaningful moment -- his to give
    hers to receive -- and appreciate anew
        her dalliance forgotten, worn but better --
            the newly experienced princess grateful
                to become one in their timeless slime less
                NOW

Ah yes, the <u>excel</u> eration and <u>excite</u> ment of that never-to-be-forgotten first meeting! Who can say it was not 'Kismet'?

THE EXCITEMENT OF MEETING HER

The Sleep-Thief surreptitiously scampers away to think
    with mid-night robbery of another like-gold precious wink
        then evaporates in the mists of light blue pre-dawn

mind provokes & pokes thoughts that replicate & duplicate
    the morrow's travel details - charge and enlarge pointlessly
        excessive uncalled surplus factors ad infinitum tirelessly

superfluous redundant thought datum continues uninterrupted
    anticipation's exhilaration shrill voice masks needed zzzs
        veils of thrills elude a tranquil mind & births a beehive of
buzzings

embrace the flow & sweet plea of vigilant alerting adrenaline
    as exciting stimulating pleasure like gold fuzzy bee workers
        creating excreting the white pod-combs of sweet honey

to meet again is all that matters --- sleep be damned –
    the plot thickens adrenal glands pump up the needed oomph
        contrived 'accidental touch' portends less sleep - more sham

While the near universal belief that women are the inferior gender is refuted by contemporary scientific empirical data, the false prejudice of female inferiority -- while often emphasized in Temple, Church & Mosque – is still nurtured and promoted by inferior men the world around. The influences guided by such prejudice has led countless men to 'take women for granted' to their own ultimate detriment.

SHE SAID – ERSATZ 'HE SAID'...

Women 'on their own'
Oft well prepared
Honors graduates
Of elite women's colleges
Ersatz dreams pass

For these not unusual
But special women
Faux Spinsterhood is as expected
As a full blown coronary
Ersatz imaginings

Their dreams collect after dark
While staring up or out silently
Waiting -- yes and more waiting
Then he arrives and she says yes
Ersatz prince charming

But Silent and soundlessness
Become the operative words
In excepted unexpected liaison
Who knew? Everyone!
Ersatz wisdom

Even with scheduled cuddles
Her 'He' has no lexis of affection
Only orgasmic grunts & grimaces
Then predictable silence & sleep
Ersatz her satisfaction

Her mate dozes alongside
Like a horrific quasi-animated
Ruddy brick stuck in a muddy riverbed
Snoring, snorting with the superficial
Ersatz her contentment

Together they slide wordlessly
Toward the 'golden contentment'
Of their soundless sixties
She intuits a bleak end to
Ersatz 'Spinster's' tale?

The one consistent 'flaw' that most women appear to possess ... is the seeming genetic disposition to 'care' with heart fullness.

THE HEART KNOWS

Is knowing by heart
learning by rote memory
　mere projections of what was?
　Or Is "only with heart" -- one
　can know oneness
　　Life's Wholeness

She "knows you by heart"
perhaps better than you
　because her heart
　Is less critical
　　less judgmental
　　less divisive

Our world's not of dualism
It is "only with heart"
　that one sees one!
　To "know by heart"
　is to practice
　　The Heart's Oneness

To know by heart
Is to know the concord
　of nature's unity
　Every life requires
　a full measure of loss
　　Hello requires Goodbye

To know by heart
Is to know life's harmony
　and the wasting of time
　with a 'rose' or 'being' when
　feeling and smelling are one!
　Trickster minds create duality

Besides huge measures of forgiveness and gratitude, Lasting relationships appear to contain, among other qualities, two essentials: <u>communication 'transparency'</u> and mutually satisfying <u>physical intimacy</u>.

LOVE IS FORBEARANCE

I ask not that you be god
Or even be good
Or write love poems
Or calming sonnets

Only allow your soft underbelly
To pose then expose your truth
As the desert sands must insist
Clouds burst & release their tears

Then let dryness roll away unabated
Absorbed by an impatient audience
of thirsty eager Truth-Sayers
Offering themselves back again

I ask not that you be a goddess
Or even a half human demigod
Or speak eloquently of love
Or make overtures of merging

Such is the never-ending cycle
in love's uncovered forbearance
And the revealed human mystery.
In such exposure -- we triumph

And of course, within this category of poems, sometimes a 'blind date' at a dreamy Palm Springs restaurant-retreat, is required...

BLIND DATE APPARITION

Days of 'Spring' were passing fast
As into my fixed gaze was cast
A prize whose glossy skin now shown
With glistening light and amber glow
My unbelieving stare was not to show

But still I reeled in the noonday heat
Beholding her with a dizzy heart beat
And quietly still, I sought some relief
From the frail fracas of memory repeats
Of her as a dream I held in disbelief

In stylish 'mid-century's' I saw the lights
From LED and lasers, light did zip
Revealing then her visage ever so bright
Immersed by Vallauris' flecked Ficus light
Still, no commitment escaped her lips

Yet there behind her chic stylish pose
I 'saw' a veto waiting in hidden repose
Her wide wish revealed by wiggling toes
And behind her proud and stuck-up nose
My mini-wish: 'someday she'd not say no'

METAPHORS of ICELAND

*My spontaneous journey to Iceland was filled with awe and wonder.
These Nordic people have carved a 'Shangri-La' from a remote,
seemingly inhospitable island.*

*One of the last items on my "Bucket List" was to view the Aurora
Borealis or Northern Lights. Even after spending four months in
Alaska the "Lights" eluded me. Thus, as my seasons pass more
quickly than ever before, I felt an urgency and since a visit to Iceland
in late Autumn is almost guaranteed a sight – I took the chance and
sure enough, I was rewarded with a whole lot more.*

Mt. Hekla is the best-known volcano of Iceland. It is situated approx 120miles northeast of Reykjavik. The first documented eruption took place in 1104, followed by further outbreaks in 1693 and 1766-1768. The ash devastated pastures and the gases poisoned the herds. The most recent outbreak started on February 26th 2000, lasting 11 days. Most of the ashes covered mostly uninhabited areas; a small part fell on the northern inhabited part of Iceland. The ash (tephra. which is actually airborne volcanic dust,) absorbs fluoride and gaseous silica on its surface. The delicate particles are then blown away further; and by having a larger surface area they absorb more fluorides.

Fluorides are water-soluble and quickly dissolve from the 'tephra' into the groundwater. They are the toxic part of the ash and cause the poisoning and subsequent death of the grazing animals. Feeding on the ash on the pasture grasses causes formation of crystals on teeth and deposits in stomach and intestines.

Homeopathic Physicians consider minute amounts to be beneficial to human health—analogous to the way many vaccinations are considered helpful,

TAK TAK* ICELAND LAVA—

Iceland lava flows to virgin mountainsides
snaps, spews and slithers leisurely downward
baptizing itself in frigid frosty glacial sea side

Tak Tak Hekla

above the busy bustle of Reykjavik's harbor show
macabre ash pollution injects an uncanny sky glow
tinges sunrises and sunsets with an eerie color flow

Tak Tak Hekla

Still glowing newly forming would-be hot pots
crackle like crisp crusty bubbling blubber gut
churn char and mar Gaia's melting mantle

Tak Tak Hekla

powder like micro fecal filth from Earth's bowel
seize, seethe, & leave blankets of black bitter foul
sky-grime spreads poison gossip silent owl

Tak Tak Hekla

eight weeks unbiased ground fissures spew fizz & flow
wheezing gases spurt -spread across countryside glow
prayer-pleas nary rejoin in towering Hallgrímskirkja

Tak Tak Hekla

Just another day for solid Viking Iceland citizen's lot
Anna rebuilds barns -- as Occam demands -- or not
Ancient heritage passes on the stout genes of hardiness

Tak Tak Hekla

*TAK TAK = thank you

Back to 1918 - the wives and daughters of the Westman Islands, (far-flung archipelago off of Iceland's remote southern coast,) grew tired of losing their sailor husbands and fathers to the sea.

They organized, forming what would become the first ICE-SAR rescue team:

Iceland has a small police force and a minor coast guard; no army or anyone else who can step up. In almost every town and village ICE SAR primarily focused on rescuing sailors from stranded ships. The scope expanded with need, today driven in particular by the country's growing tourist industry and thus the growing need for adroit heroes.

Eighty percent of the country is uninhabited, and there a number of ways to get lost or stuck. Today, there are 100 ICE-SAR search and rescue teams capable of handling everything from high-mountain glacier rescues to volcanic eruptions. They also maintain a network of huts, scattered across Iceland, where travelers can seek refuge during emergencies and create still more heroic stories.

VIKINGS LEGENDS & SAVOIR FAIRE

Bloody Erik lived to see his 'Red' feats go down as superstar
Explorer- warrior extraordinaire - slaughtered without a care
his celebrity name did ring as Iceland's famous Viking
Do people need heroes and myths more than savoir-faire?

Today modern photo and Icelandic Commission confirms
Lagarfljótsormur Mythical Sea Monster Actually seen real
YES, Vivid Videos attracts tourists by the boatload to thrill
To See "frozen fish net" squiggling motion moving with zeal

Still ICE SAR volunteers do what needs to be done in remote area
two Americans + two Canadians a winter road trip – out of luck
In one single skittering second joined some who lack brainpower
Namely tourists who underrate Iceland and get hopelessly stuck

Yearly hundreds of tourists, rescued in Iceland's countryside
merciless mocking glow of the gauge note gas tank's impending
emptiness.
Naive visitors in Iceland more often than not require emergency
interest
It's 6 p.m. on Xmas day, which means darkness arrived as nemesis

ICE-SAR rescues French couple – obvious warning sign shun sandstorm blew out car windows, allowing near- death bluster. Iceland's rapidly deteriorating weather led five <u>Picnickers</u>' fun to iceberg perfect lunch locale was pushed to sea by wind twister

Thus it begins -- heroic yet exaggerated stories become myths
People need heroes* -- children need legends, dreams and fantasy
Even remote Iceland has its share of Clauses, Bunnies and Fairies
Apparently people need heroes and myths more than savior-faire?

* Icelander Mr. Hafthor Biornasson stands 6'9" and weighs in at 430 lbs and will no doubt continue his successful march to being titled the official worlds-strongest –Viking.
Biornasson like some of his Viking forebears is for real and will one day no doubt become a legend.
Yes, many so called *sapiens* apparently still need "heroes' and tooth fairies.

Myths and religious-like stories, most often lead to misconception, or to sophomoric, pedantic, and delusional mind-sets. Ideologies and so-called "heresies" are formulated from fabrication albeit fantasy – usually from childhood. I'm always astounded by the many people who have attempted to instruct me on the merits of "faith" or "believe in something" -- by this they usually mean a legend or myth taught to them by a previous generation.

AURORA -- VALHALLA LINK OR?

The Aurora Borealis
 dazzling light for Vikings
  dead warrior's private path
   glistening heavenward
    from earth to Asgard

Aurora also linked
 To dead virgins
  Brushing Upwards
   Sparks of first sex
    with dead warriors

Then refracting reflections
 of Virgin shining Shields
  leading warriors To Valhalla
   Valkyries of heavenly mists
    Unending vibration queue

Currently know Sun Spots and
  Solar winds interact
   At earth's magnetic poles
    Charged space particles
     collide with Gaia's dazzling derma

Myths and magic still link
  To primitive intellect
   Still prevails among
    Gaia negligent believers
     Who Deny factual curiosity

October 2014

MISCELLANEOUS METAPHORS

The following poems, in my mind, did not fit the general category divisions I had outlined -- thus a miscellaneous ...

Meditation is one of those human experiences that some attempt to define and put into boundaries of particular paradigms. However...

DAY OFF

Being still & quiet
Unlike being motionless
Can be meditation
I can ride a bicycle
Or run a marathon
While still and quiet

I can take the day off
And be still and quiet
Stillness is different
Than stationary
To act is action
Stillness is silence

Kneeling can be exploitive
Sitting can be a verb
Meditation can be action
Silence also requires a deed
One-ness wants silence
Meditation can be that

OR more
OR less

My Ozzy sheepdog was obviously born the 'runt' of the litter on a working cattle ranch. It seems he needed rescuing ... and so I brought him home where I made some other discoveries:

MR DUGAN

Sheep dog is too tame a name
for Mr Dugan -- sheepish also impish
sentry guard -- compassionate pal
 More like kith & kin with tail
   Unconditional love
     Undying devotion
        Perennial 'pay it forward'
        Ceaselessly forgiving
rescued from abuse
previously impaired:
by fly swatter,
  by broom
    by children
undoubtedly
constrained
  by fear &
    cruel conditioning
      during his puppyhood

Mr D came into my life
disabled by sheepish fear
of swatters, brooms, and kids
he can now do naught more
than bark heartily
at approaching strangers
(usually behind me or closed screen door)
with wrinkled nose as warning precursor
sometimes a pseudo nip as ersatz assault

Mr Dugan struggles not to hide
when his perceived childhood offenders
(swatters, brooms, kids)
show up for
 swatting at pesky flies
  sweeping floors
   teaching adults

His girlfriend Coco dramatically shows
feigned indifference to his theatrics
their rubbing
and sniffing game
crossing necks
Without respite
then surrender
when humans cease to admire

Personally, I experience 'curiosity' for new understanding as absolutely vital for human growth. Being in 'awe' of objectively determined new facts is definitely essential to spirituality... the problem comes when subjective self-delusion forms the starting point -- Just as masturbation becomes the 'beginning and end' for some, so subjective illusions can also dominate human life.

CURIOSITY

Popular & Prevailing popular life advice—
"follow your passion"
Popular & prevalent because it sounds wise
However
authentic wise-ones pursue
curiosity -- not passion.

First problem: easier said than done.
In order to follow citified/certified qualified passion
we spend far too much in/on frantic goose-chase.
In order to follow citified/certified qualified passion –
The other problem becomes: need to find IT

Here's where most zealots need help:
—forget about passion,
---follow your curiosity:
---passion is a one-night-stand.
---passion's hot, it burns -- you can't access that every day …

Every single day
 there's an objective something to be curious about
—follow it,
it's a clue,
it leads to epiphanies of awe
echoing
--- Einstein "I own no special talent - only passionate curiosity."
--- Steve Jobs: "what I stumble into is by following my curiosity …"

*The recent success of Portugal's drug laws should be "reason enough!" ***

JEOPARDOUS ASSUMPTION:

Consuming marijuana weed
  alleged comparable to cocktails
    Cautious 'political' PCs impede
      ill informed 'fundies' now lead

Marijuana the "devil weed" maxim
  bragged the ancient dictum bore
    This pop propped - ganja truism
      Waxed high in the twenties roar

Yet facts and acts remain -- clear impression
  Homo 'wise one's' Alcohol ingestion
    kills three & a half million each annotation
      more than annual AIDS, & gun utilization

World Health Organization cautious admonition
  cool nonchalant caveats casually warn
    WHO's Mental Health factual verbalization
      one alcohol death each ten secs is born

Substance Abuse health caution is clear
  tells Geneva reporters who appear
    Afghan heroin poppies thrive near here
      While wealthy Imams behead and cheer

Old school brain-dead neurons roil
  sipping (gulping) Scotch & Martini
    & Burn the organic cana-ban-glean
      deaf ears listen to factual scene

I've often wondered about selective picking over scriptural readings and hearing only what fits into one's preconceived notions:

BIBLE ICONIC INJUNCTIONS

I too can be discriminating
   Opting bible verses:
"Ye must be born again"
   is awfully special!
Initially neo-born helplessness
   Depend on "Ma" & "Aba"
and "out-there" nurturing
   Icons–a-birthin'

New-borne employ emotional
   crying, pleading
(praying) receiving comfort via
   myths and heroes
The Santa Clause allotment
   Easter bunny too
Yes tooth fairy to boot
   More Iconic origins

"When I was neipos (*gr.* neo-born)*
    I thought as a child
I spake as a child,
    I felt as a child,
I reasoned as a child"
    (an old acorn
proxy for 'wanna-be' profundity)
    Who said Iconic?

When Awakened "Born again"
    put away childish logic
grow out of emotional fixation
    allow logic & reason
cure childhood addictive fix
    to naive gullibility--
        BE Iconoclastic?

*nēpios—(Greek) denotes properly a baby, an infant.
When we advance to wakening and awareness -- we lay aside, as unworthy of
our attention, to the views, feelings, we had as 'nepios' children coming out of the
womb (myth fixation) being birthed again accepting response-ability rather than
dependency on myth.
See I Corinthians 13-11

It seems that Oregon now offers a dignified alternative:

DIGNIFIED DEATH DECISION?

I know - I know, Dylan said "rage - rage"
and all that hypocritical poetic crap
Now if I link IT with ecclesia & holy sin
& Create a perfect tasteless cocktail
to prop up my body's empty scarecrow
and the dying light

Other human ideals do triumph!
Others campaign for dignified death
freedom to ingest another cocktail
Others offer legal lethal right to die
claim noble rights over one's destiny
and the dying light

As such - popular laws assert life
-- publically explicitly - privately implicitly --
pressure the disabled, chronically sick
to do "decent, dignified thing"-- depart!
"right to die" then morphs to "*expectation*"
and the dying light

if 'dignity' is operational
& 'quality of life' significant
then choice is conscionable for *me*
although if faith always triumphs
and "belief" my only choice— then
"the dying light" is <u>not mine to choose</u> *

(*see: *free will* by S. Harris)

"Losing a belief in free will has not made me a fatalist - in fact, it has increased my feelings of freedom. My hopes, fears, and neuroses seem less personal and indelible. There is no telling how much I might change in the future. Just as one wouldn't draw a lasting conclusion about oneself on the basis of a brief experience of indigestion... Becoming sensitive to the background causes of one's thoughts and feelings can -paradoxically- allow for greater creative control over one's life. This understanding reveals you to be a biochemical puppet, of course, but it also allows you to grab hold of one of your strings."

"A puppet is free as long as he loves his strings."

"Many seem to have fetish of individualism. With absolutely no awareness of how fortunate one must be to succeed at anything in life, no matter how hard one works. One must be lucky to be able to work. One must be lucky to be intelligent, physically healthy, and not bankrupted in middle age by the illness of a spouse."

— Sam Harris, Free Will

www.ingramcontent.com/pod-product-compliance
Lightning Source LLC
Chambersburg PA
CBHW020532290526
45786CB00002B/839